ANCIENT WORLDS

TRAVEL BACK IN TIME AND DISCOVER THE FIRST GREAT CIVILIZATIONS

WRITTEN BY
JUSTINE WILLIS

DK LONDON
Senior Editor Michelle Crane
Senior Art Editor Rachael Grady
Writer and Researcher Justine Willis
Senior US Editor Megan Douglass
Senior Production Editor Andy Hilliard
Senior Production Controller Poppy David
Jacket Design Development Manager Sophia MTT
Managing Editor Francesca Baines
Managing Art Editor Philip Letsu
Publisher Andrew Macintyre
Associate Publishing Director Liz Wheeler
Art Director Karen Self
Publishing Director Jonathan Metcalf

DK DELHI
Senior Jacket Designer Suhita Dharamjit
DTP Designer Deepak Mittal
Senior Jackets Coordinator Priyanka Sharma Saddi

Illustrators Peter Bull, Chris @ KJA Artists,
Sofian Moumene

Consultants Peter Chrisp; Josh Emmitt; Jacob Field; Professor Joann
Fletcher; Professor Elizabeth Graham; Henry Hurst; Dr. Sushma Jansari;
Stephen Kay, FSA; William Lindesay, OBE; Professor Lloyd Llewellyn-Jones;
Professor Bill Sillar; David Stuttard; Robin Walker

First American Edition, 2024
Published in the United States by DK Publishing
A Division of Penguin Random House LLC
1745 Broadway, 20th Floor, New York, NY 10019

Copyright © 2024
Dorling Kindersley Limited
24 25 26 27 28 10 9 8 7 6 5 4 3 2 1
001–339328–April/2024

A catalog record for this book is available from the Library of Congress.
ISBN 978-0-7440-9289-9

DK books are available at special discounts when purchased in bulk
for sales promotions, premiums, fund-raising, or educational use.
For details, contact: DK Publishing Special Markets,
1745 Broadway, 20th Floor, New York, NY 10019
SpecialSales@dk.com

Printed and bound in China

www.dk.com

Smithsonian

MIX
Paper | Supporting
responsible forestry
FSC™ C018179

This book was made with Forest
Stewardship Council™ certified
paper—one small step in DK's
commitment to a sustainable future.
Learn more at
www.dk.com/uk/information/sustainability

CONTENTS

Ancient Worlds

The earliest civilizations sprang up along
major rivers in Mesopotamia (modern-day Iraq)
and China. Over time, many more emerged all
over the world. This book re-creates scenes
from 12 ancient worlds in Africa, the Americas,
Asia, Europe, and Oceania. The location of
each one is shown on this map.

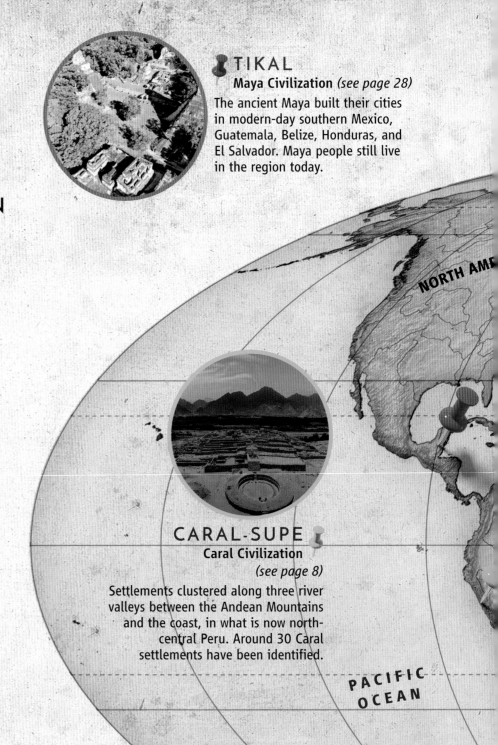

TIKAL
Maya Civilization *(see page 28)*
The ancient Maya built their cities
in modern-day southern Mexico,
Guatemala, Belize, Honduras, and
El Salvador. Maya people still live
in the region today.

NORTH AME

CARAL-SUPE
Caral Civilization
(see page 8)
Settlements clustered along three river
valleys between the Andean Mountains
and the coast, in what is now north-
central Peru. Around 30 Caral
settlements have been identified.

PACIFIC
OCEAN

CARTHAGE
Carthaginian Civilization
(see page 22)
The port city of Carthage was in modern-day
Tunisia. At its most powerful, Carthage
controlled Mediterranean trading ports all
along the North African and Spanish coast.

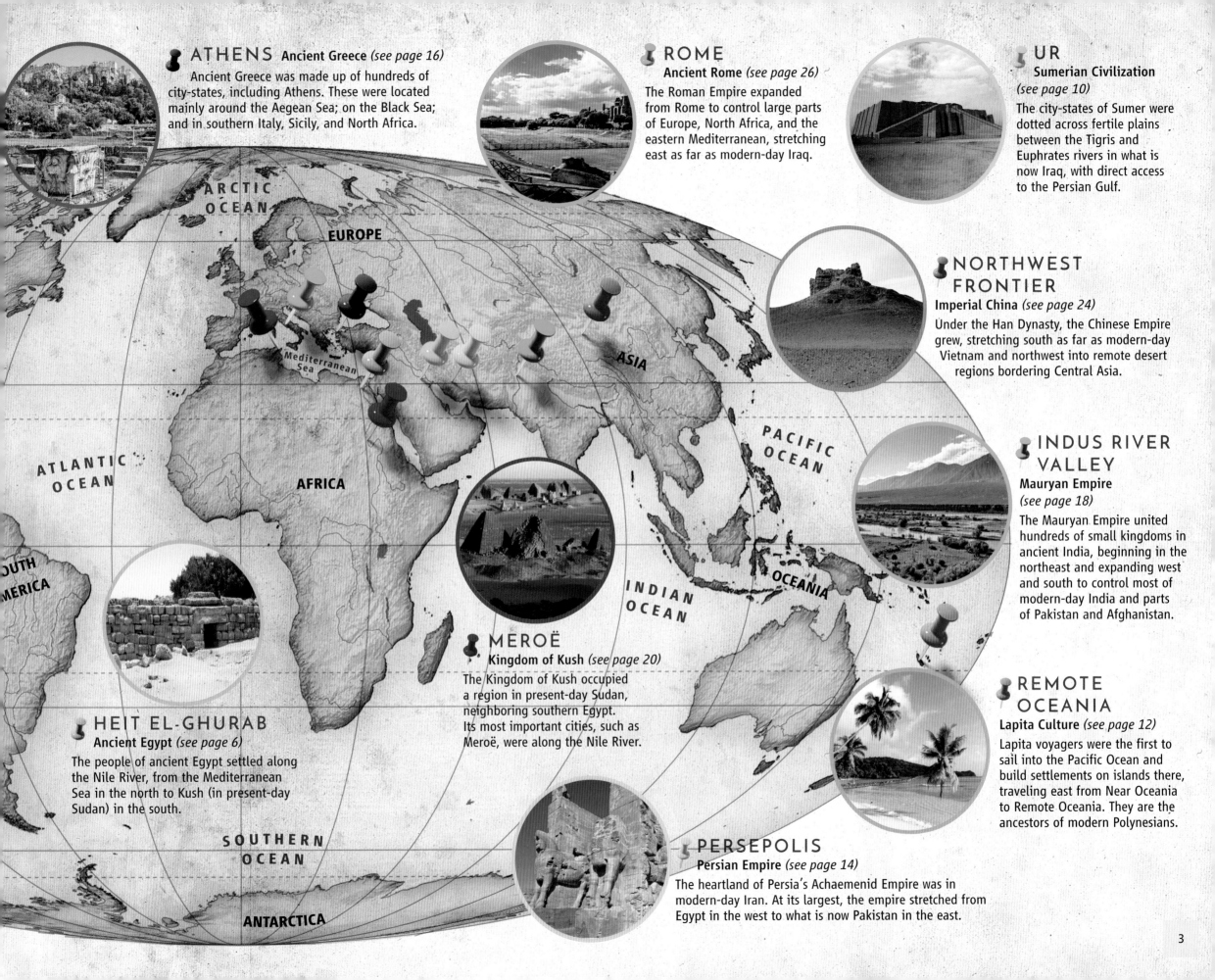

ATHENS Ancient Greece (see page 16)

Ancient Greece was made up of hundreds of city-states, including Athens. These were located mainly around the Aegean Sea; on the Black Sea; and in southern Italy, Sicily, and North Africa.

ROME
Ancient Rome (see page 26)

The Roman Empire expanded from Rome to control large parts of Europe, North Africa, and the eastern Mediterranean, stretching east as far as modern-day Iraq.

UR
Sumerian Civilization (see page 10)

The city-states of Sumer were dotted across fertile plains between the Tigris and Euphrates rivers in what is now Iraq, with direct access to the Persian Gulf.

NORTHWEST FRONTIER
Imperial China (see page 24)

Under the Han Dynasty, the Chinese Empire grew, stretching south as far as modern-day Vietnam and northwest into remote desert regions bordering Central Asia.

INDUS RIVER VALLEY
Mauryan Empire (see page 18)

The Mauryan Empire united hundreds of small kingdoms in ancient India, beginning in the northeast and expanding west and south to control most of modern-day India and parts of Pakistan and Afghanistan.

MEROË
Kingdom of Kush (see page 20)

The Kingdom of Kush occupied a region in present-day Sudan, neighboring southern Egypt. Its most important cities, such as Meroë, were along the Nile River.

REMOTE OCEANIA
Lapita Culture (see page 12)

Lapita voyagers were the first to sail into the Pacific Ocean and build settlements on islands there, traveling east from Near Oceania to Remote Oceania. They are the ancestors of modern Polynesians.

HEIT EL-GHURAB
Ancient Egypt (see page 6)

The people of ancient Egypt settled along the Nile River, from the Mediterranean Sea in the north to Kush (in present-day Sudan) in the south.

PERSEPOLIS
Persian Empire (see page 14)

The heartland of Persia's Achaemenid Empire was in modern-day Iran. At its largest, the empire stretched from Egypt in the west to what is now Pakistan in the east.

ARCTIC OCEAN

EUROPE

ASIA

ATLANTIC OCEAN

Mediterranean Sea

AFRICA

PACIFIC OCEAN

SOUTH AMERICA

INDIAN OCEAN

OCEANIA

SOUTHERN OCEAN

ANTARCTICA

4

YELLOW RIVER CIVILIZATION
c. 7000–c. 1400 BCE

Many experts believe the very first Chinese villages sprang up in the Yellow River Valley.

'AIN GHAZAL
c. 7200–c. 5000 BCE

The villagers of 'Ain Ghazal (in modern-day Jordan) began as hunter-gatherers, but gradually became farmers.

MAYA CIVILIZATION
c. 2000 BCE–c. 900 CE

The early Maya lived in farming villages but, as the population grew, cities developed, each ruled by a king. The most famous Maya art, buildings, and writing are from the Classic Period (c. 250–c. 900 CE).

see page 28

SUMERIAN CIVILIZATION
c. 5000–c. 1750 BCE

The Sumerians are believed to have built the world's first cities in Mesopotamia, including monumental stepped temples. They invented many things adopted by later civilizations, such as the wheel and the first known writing, called cuneiform.

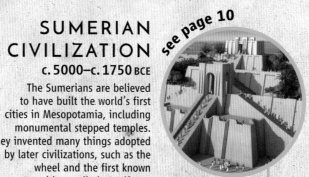
see page 10

MINOAN CIVILIZATION
c. 2800–c. 1100 BCE

The Minoans were talented artists and developed their own writing. They lived on the island of Crete.

INDUS RIVER CIVILIZATION
c. 2600–c. 1700 BCE

The well-planned cities built by Indus people in the region of modern-day Pakistan and India were among the world's earliest.

THE ÇATALHÖYÜK SETTLEMENT
c. 7500–c. 5700 BCE

At Çatalhöyük, in modern-day Turkey (Türkiye), improvements in farming helped people to settle and build towns.

MOUND BUILDERS
c. 3500 BCE–c. 1000 CE

The eastern United States is dotted with striking earthen mounds built for burial and religious reasons by Indigenous peoples.

65,000 BCE   6500 BCE   4500 BCE   2500 BCE

FIRST NATIONS AUSTRALIANS
c. 65,000 BCE

The ancestors of today's Aboriginal Australians were Australia's first people. They were skilled hunter-gatherers and renowned for their artistic traditions.

LINEAR POTTERY CULTURE
c. 5500–c. 4600 BCE

The first farmers in Central Europe lived in villages near rivers. They decorated their pottery with lines.

CARAL CIVILIZATION
c. 3500–c. 1800 BCE

The Caral Civilization (sometimes called Norte Chico) is the oldest in the Americas. While pyramid-builders were at work in Egypt, Caral people were constructing pyramid-shaped buildings of their own, used as public buildings and temples.

see page 8

ASSYRIAN EMPIRE
c. 2000–c. 600 BCE

The Assyrians, based in Mesopotamia, were known for their advanced fighting methods and iron weapons.

YANGTZE CIVILIZATION
c. 7000–c. 2000 BCE

Some of China's earliest farming communities settled along the Yangtze River, attracted by its fertile soil.

ANCIENT CHINA
c. 2000–c. 220 BCE

In this period, powerful families brought communities under their rule, creating separate kingdoms within China.

ANCIENT EGYPT
c. 3100–c. 30 BCE

Ancient Egypt was one of the greatest ancient civilizations. Its rulers, the pharaohs, had the wealth and power to organize the building of grand pyramids and beautifully decorated temples to honor themselves and their gods.

see page 6

BABYLONIAN EMPIRE
c. 2000–539 BCE

The Babylonians ruled Mesopotamia twice. Their walled capital, Babylon, had beautiful temples and gardens.

CIVILIZATIONS THROUGH TIME

The 12 scenes in this book show just some of the many civilizations that developed around the world in ancient times. This timeline shows when each one began, how long it lasted, and which ones existed at the same time. While some flourished on their own, others met and traded goods and ideas with each other.

MYCENAEAN CIVILIZATION
c. 1600–c. 1100 BCE

The Mycenaeans were a rich, powerful people living in Greece. They were known as good soldiers and traders.

see page 20

KINGDOM OF KUSH
c. 800 BCE–c. 320 CE

The land of Kush had gold and iron mines, and grew wealthy through trade with nearby regions, including Egypt. Kushite kings ruled ancient Egypt as pharaohs for a time, and their peoples shared similar beliefs and customs.

see page 18

MAURYAN EMPIRE
c. 321–c. 185 BCE

The Mauryan kings united many small kingdoms to create the first Indian Empire. The first ruler, Chandragupta, used his awe-inspiring army to grow the empire, while the third, Ashoka, became a Buddhist and encouraged peaceful behavior.

KINGDOM OF AKSUM
c. 100–c. 1000 CE

From their capital in modern-day Ethiopia, the kings of Aksum ruled a powerful trading empire.

PHOENICIAN CIVILIZATION
c. 1500–c. 300 BCE

The Phoenicians were clever shipbuilders and merchants who founded trading ports all around the Mediterranean Sea.

see page 22

CARTHAGINIAN EMPIRE
c. 800–146 BCE

Carthage was founded by the Phoenicians, and Carthaginians inherited their trading and shipbuilding skills, building a wealthy trading empire. The Romans were jealous, and waged war against Carthage three times, eventually destroying it.

GUPTA CIVILIZATION
c. 320–c. 550 CE

Under the Gupta rulers of northern India there were important developments in art and architecture.

1000 BCE   500 BCE   50 CE

OLMECS
c. 1200–c. 400 BCE

The pyramids and sculptures of the Olmecs, in modern-day Mexico, probably influenced other civilizations in the region, such as the Maya.

ANCESTRAL PUEBLO
c. 100–c. 1600 CE

Ancestral Pueblo people in the southwestern United States built houses high on cliff faces.

LAPITA CULTURE
c. 1500–c. 400 BCE

The Lapita used the sun, stars, and ocean currents to guide them as they explored the Pacific Ocean, discovering islands and building settlements there. As well as hunting and gathering food, they also kept animals.

see page 12

see page 16

ANCIENT GREECE
c. 800–31 BCE

The ancient Greeks developed new ways of ruling and thinking about life. Their ideas about politics, science, math, art, and architecture have shaped the way people in many countries live today.

PERSIAN EMPIRE
c. 550–c. 334 BCE

The Achaemenid kings of Persia were famous for living in luxury, but they were also clever rulers. They kept in regular contact with their subject nations and showed them respect, making it easier to control their vast empire.

see page 26
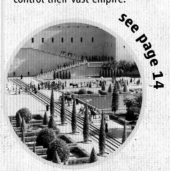

ANCIENT ROME
c. 509 BCE–1453 CE

The ancient Romans built the largest, most powerful empire the world had ever seen. By 285 CE, it had grown too big to manage effectively, so it was divided into two parts: Western and Eastern. The Western Empire ended in 476 CE, while the Eastern (Byzantine) Empire continued until 1453.

IMPERIAL CHINA
c. 220 BCE–1912 CE

In imperial times, China was ruled by a series of royal families (dynasties). The Han emperors (202 BCE–220 CE) strongly influenced China's future, including by encouraging trade with Central Asia and the Roman Empire.

see page 24
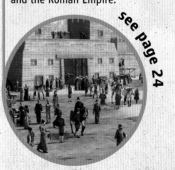

Each house has a dormitory downstairs, sleeping 40 workers side by side. A few sleep upstairs, too, to have more space.

At the gatehouses, royal scribes record the time each worker goes to and returns from work, making sure everyone has been counted.

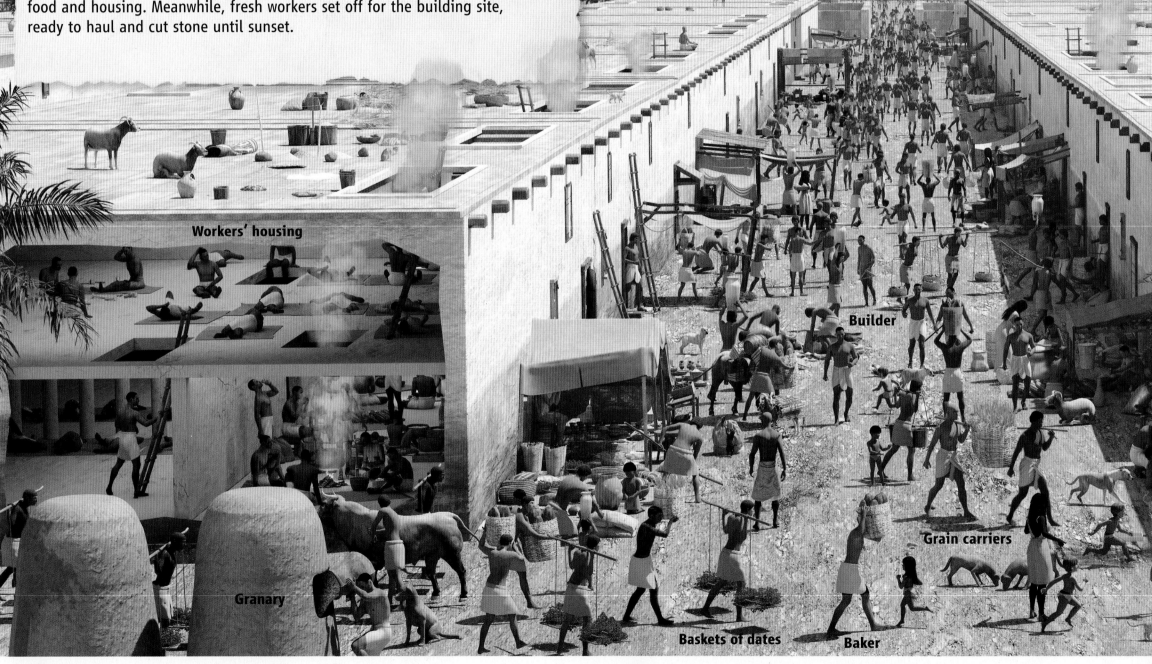

THE PYRAMID BUILDERS' TOWN
Heit el-Ghurab, Ancient Egypt, c. 2515 BCE

Block by block, the pharaoh Menkaure's pyramid climbs into the sky. His will be the third at Giza, joining those of pharaohs Khafre and Khufu. The midday sun is fierce, and the morning workers stop and stretch. They begin the walk back to Heit el-Ghurab, the town built to provide the pyramid builders with food and housing. Meanwhile, fresh workers set off for the building site, ready to haul and cut stone until sunset.

Pyramid of Menkaure (under construction)

Gatehouse

Workers' housing

Builder

Grain carriers

Granary

Baskets of dates

Baker

These men are cooking fish stew in their shared kitchen. One chops onions and garlic ready to add to the pot.

A man pours wheat into one of the town's many grain bins. It will be used to make beer or bread.

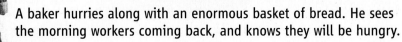
A baker hurries along with an enormous basket of bread. He sees the morning workers coming back, and knows they will be hungry.

This man's copper chisels are blunt after hours of stoneworking. He sits in the shade to sharpen them before going to rest.

This builder has been hauling stone all morning. His body aches, and he longs to rest in the cool shade of his house.

 As the afternoon workers pass through the gateway in the Wall of the Crow, they enter the sacred ground of the pyramid site.

This barge is carrying limestone from a quarry along the Nile River. It will be used for the pyramid's outer layer.

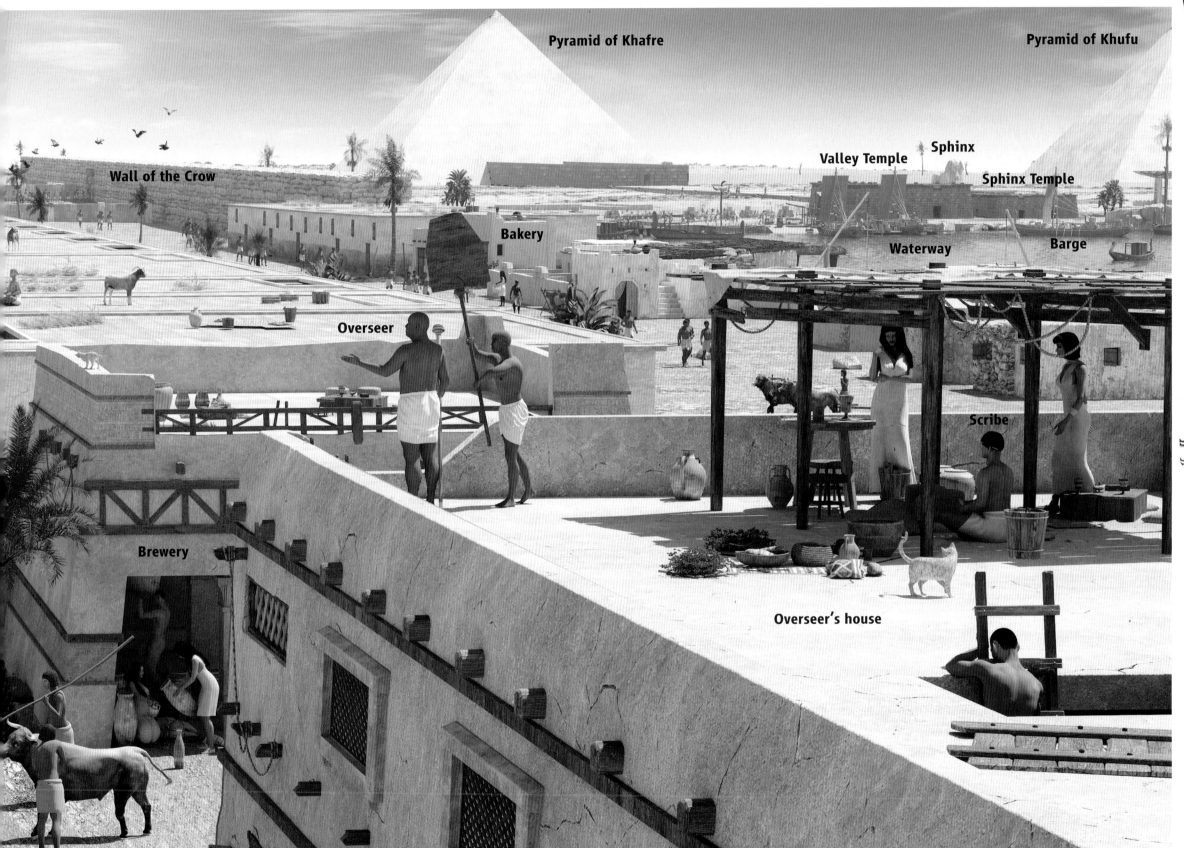

Pyramid of Khafre

Pyramid of Khufu

Sphinx

Valley Temple

Wall of the Crow

Sphinx Temple

Bakery

Waterway

Barge

Overseer

Scribe

Brewery

Overseer's house

The pharaoh's overseer watches from his rooftop, ensuring the builders are fed and work as expected.

 One of the foods provided for the workers is beef. The town has its own cattle pen, and this cow is being taken there.

 A woman pours beer into jugs to take to the thirsty workers. Beer is their main drink, so her brewery is always busy.

The Greater Pyramid is the largest and most important of the public buildings around the communal area, with a circular sunken plaza used for rituals.

This woman is carrying a large gourd in which to serve the evening meal. Gourds make good containers, so she does not need pottery.

Musicians play delicate flutes made from condor and pelican bones, filling the air with their sacred sound.

A ritual leader lights a fire in the sacred altar, around which temple workers have arranged crops as religious offerings.

Greater Pyramid

Condor

Ritual leader

Circular sunken plaza

Residential area

Altar

Whalebone stool

Official with khipu

Musicians

Old Pyramid

Llama

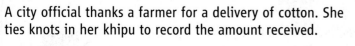
A city official thanks a farmer for a delivery of cotton. She ties knots in her khipu to record the amount received.

Using looms and needles made of animal bone, women weavers transform piles of raw cotton into cloth and fishing nets.

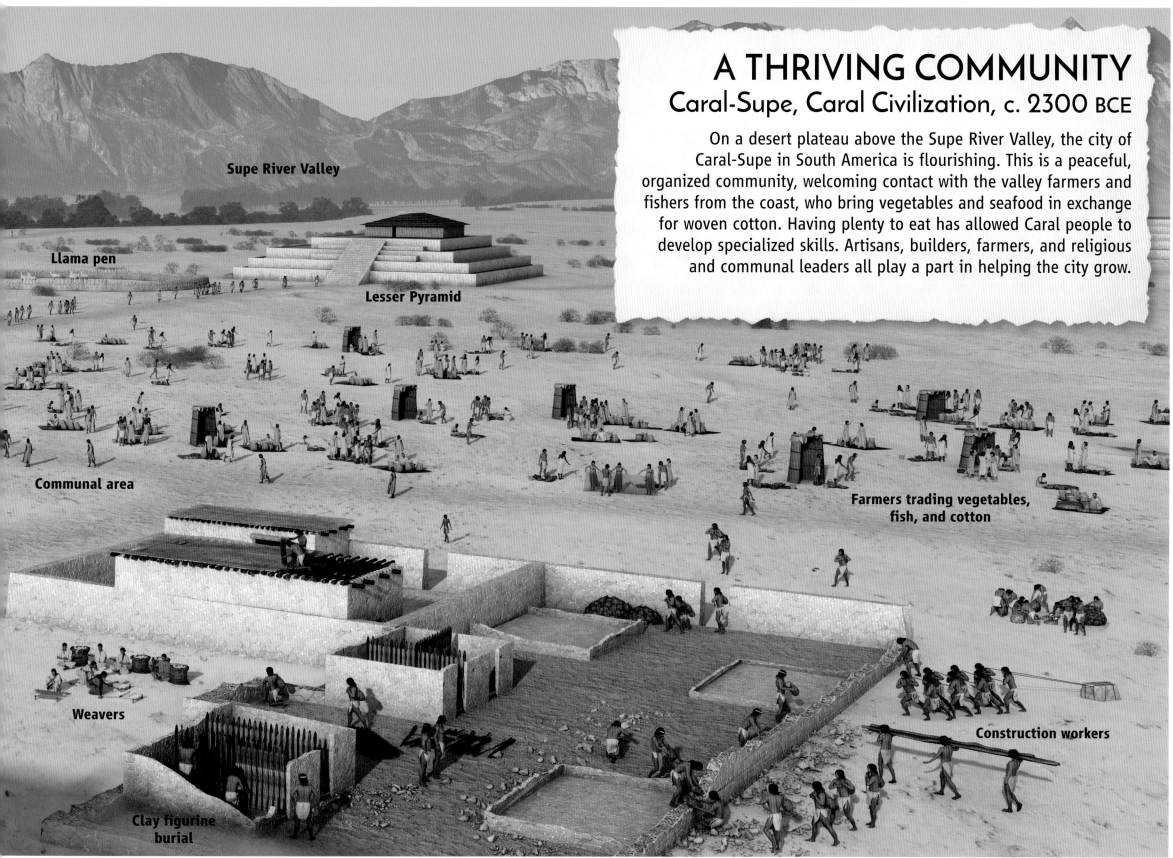

It's time to burn the household waste. A man pokes the flaming heap of shells, bones, and vegetable scraps, making them burn faster.

Men and women fill hardy shicra bags made from woven reeds with stones. These are packed into the building walls to keep them strong, even during earthquakes.

A THRIVING COMMUNITY
Caral-Supe, Caral Civilization, c. 2300 BCE

On a desert plateau above the Supe River Valley, the city of Caral-Supe in South America is flourishing. This is a peaceful, organized community, welcoming contact with the valley farmers and fishers from the coast, who bring vegetables and seafood in exchange for woven cotton. Having plenty to eat has allowed Caral people to develop specialized skills. Artisans, builders, farmers, and religious and communal leaders all play a part in helping the city grow.

Fishers from the coast offer mussels and clams in return for cotton fishing nets made by the city's skillful weavers.

A farmer trades sweet potatoes, squash, and beans grown in the fertile river valley in exchange for woven cotton.

Supe River Valley

Llama pen

Lesser Pyramid

Communal area

Farmers trading vegetables, fish, and cotton

Weavers

Construction workers

Clay figurine burial

Builders pause construction while a ritual leader buries a clay figurine inside the wall to protect the building from bad luck.

These homes will be for ritual and community leaders. Smaller houses, for less important community members, are farther away.

A shepherd herds lambs and goats into the courtyard, ready for members of the procession to take as offerings to Nanna.

Barges sail to and from the Persian Gulf, allowing Ur to trade woven cloth and leather for gold, copper, and gemstones from distant lands.

Workers rebuilding a wall use hot bitumen to set the layers of oven-baked mud bricks and make them waterproof.

A noblewoman turns her head to admire the acrobats, her golden headdress and necklaces gleaming as they catch the sun.

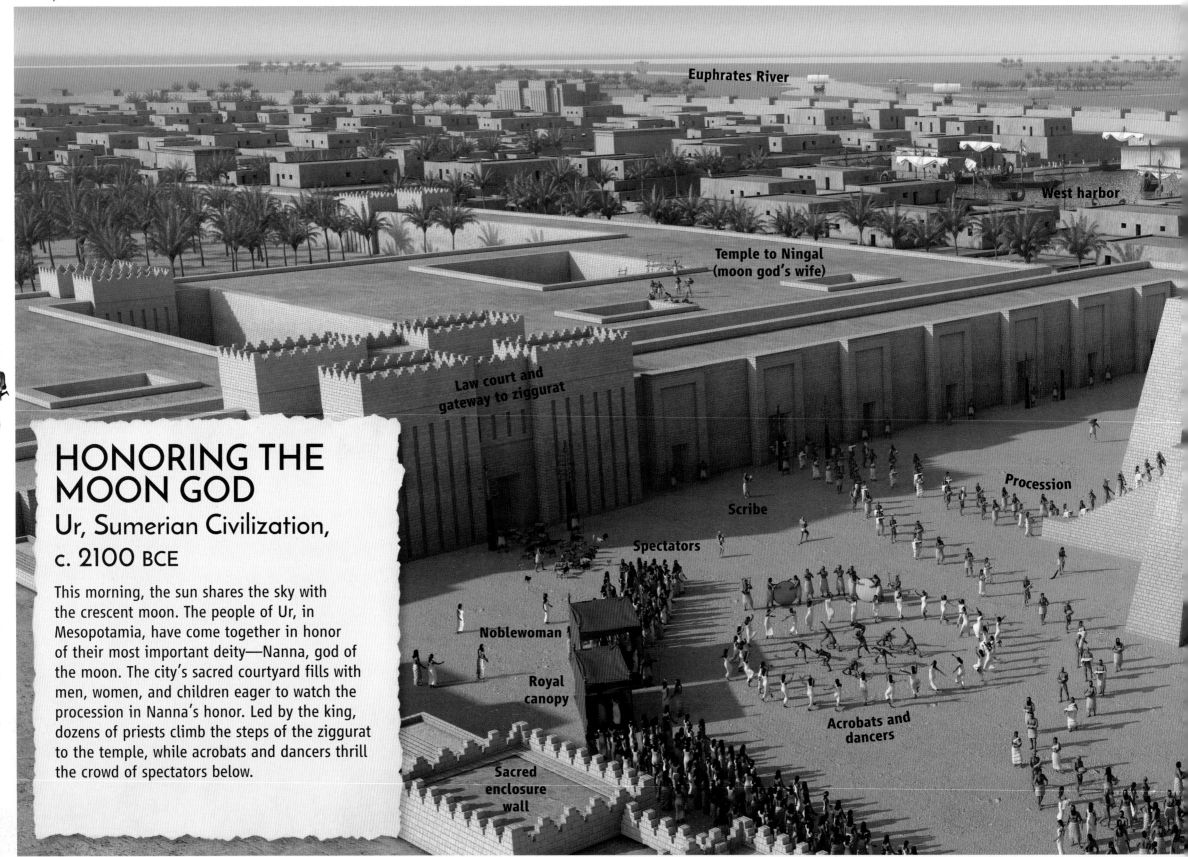

Euphrates River

West harbor

Temple to Ningal
(moon god's wife)

Law court and
gateway to ziggurat

Procession

Scribe

Spectators

Noblewoman

Royal
canopy

Acrobats and
dancers

Sacred
enclosure
wall

HONORING THE MOON GOD

Ur, Sumerian Civilization, c. 2100 BCE

This morning, the sun shares the sky with the crescent moon. The people of Ur, in Mesopotamia, have come together in honor of their most important deity—Nanna, god of the moon. The city's sacred courtyard fills with men, women, and children eager to watch the procession in Nanna's honor. Led by the king, dozens of priests climb the steps of the ziggurat to the temple, while acrobats and dancers thrill the crowd of spectators below.

Sumerian cities keep detailed records of their wealth, so scribes write down each offering leaving the temple on clay tablets, writing in cuneiform.

The music of lyres and double pipes echoes around the courtyard, growing louder and faster as the king nears the temple.

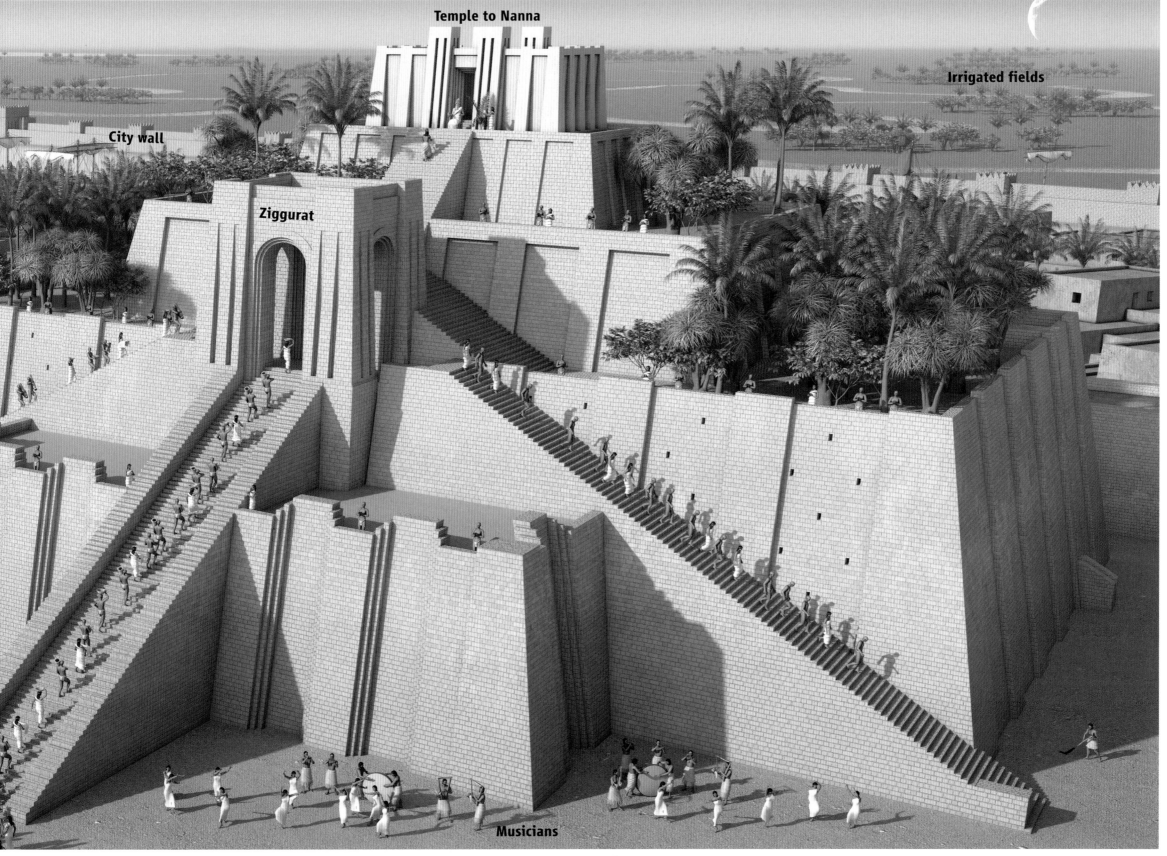

This statue of Nanna is the city's most prized treasure, and has been brought out of the temple for the ceremony.

The king's daughter is Ur's high priestess. She makes Nanna an offering of wine, pouring it into a vase filled with date-palm leaves.

Temple to Nanna

Irrigated fields

City wall

Ziggurat

Musicians

The ziggurat is sacred, and only priests and priestesses may step on it. This priest carries a drink for Nanna in a beautifully carved vase.

The king acts as the people's link to their gods. He leads the procession, carrying fresh clothes with which to dress Nanna's statue.

The ziggurat is Ur's most important religious building. Each of the three stairways to the gateway has 100 steps.

An enslaved man captured during wartime looks up from sweeping the courtyard, curious to see the procession.

Using a small, sharp piece of obsidian rock, a man gets to work slicing and cleaning a heap of freshly caught fish.

 A boy chases some chickens off the beach. The Lapita have long kept chickens and pigs, and take them when settling new islands.

A group of women weave pandanus leaves into panels, which will be sewn together to make a canoe sail.

This man is using the grooves in a shell to stamp a pattern into a decorative clay pot.

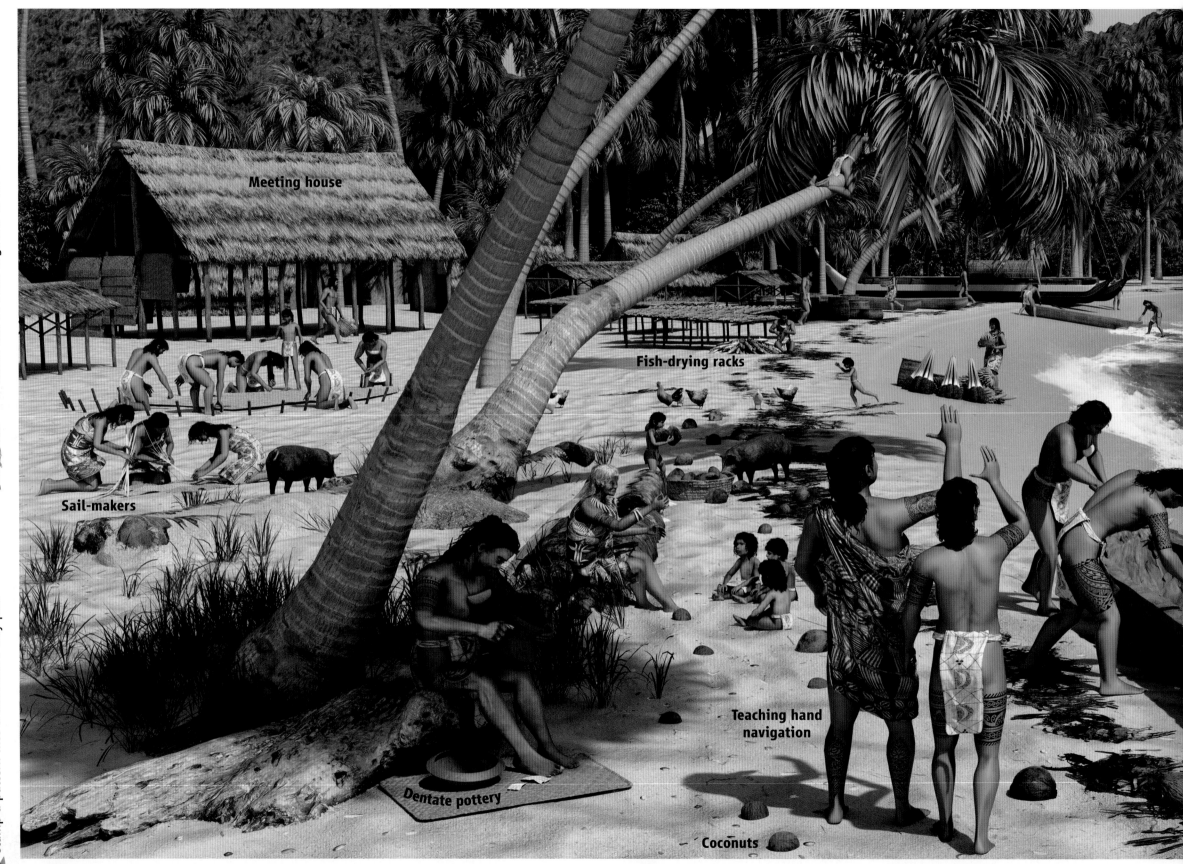

Meeting house

Fish-drying racks

Sail-makers

Teaching hand navigation

Dentate pottery

Coconuts

 A village elder thrills children with stories about her grandparents, and how they used their sailing skills to discover and settle this very island.

 This boy is learning to sail on course using hand navigation. He knows where each star rises and sets, and lines up his hand with the horizon.

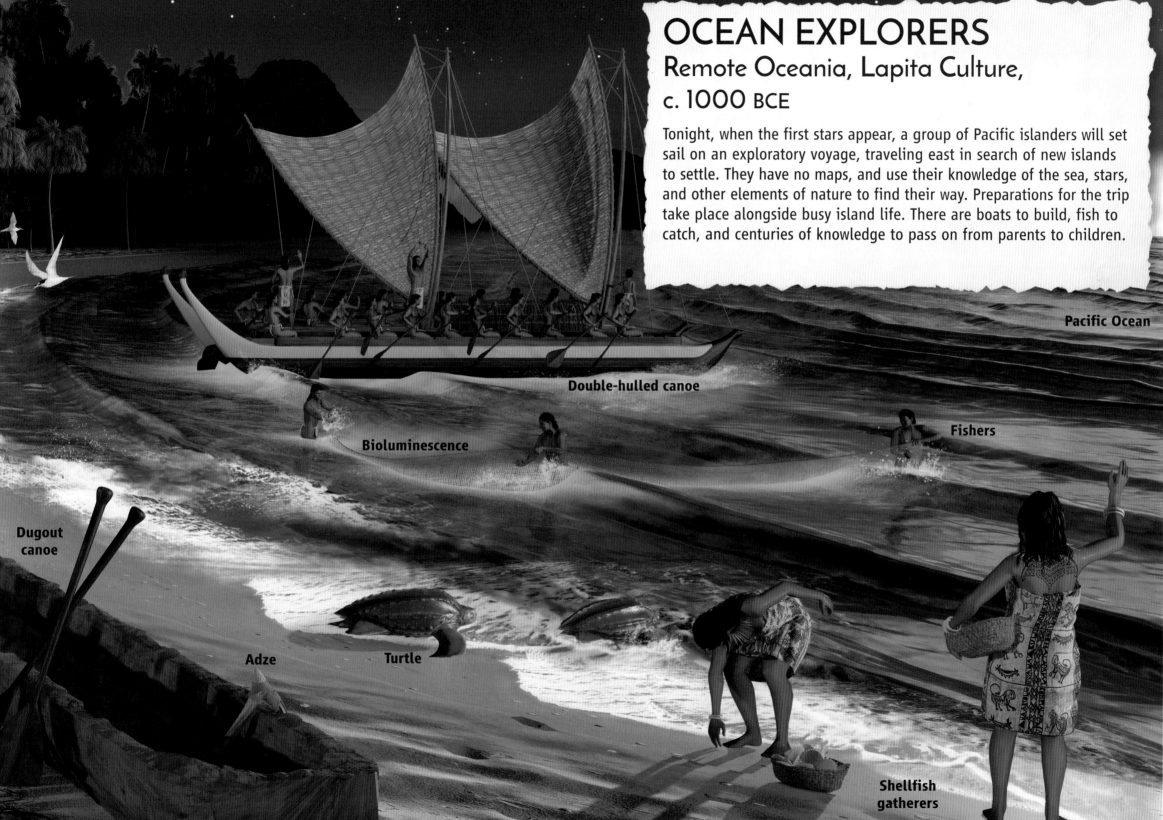

This boy is collecting coconuts. They are good to eat, and the shell fibers can be woven into rope, used to build huts and boats.

A fairy tern looks for a fish. These birds never stray far from islands, so when sailors spot them, they know land is near.

OCEAN EXPLORERS
Remote Oceania, Lapita Culture, c. 1000 BCE

Tonight, when the first stars appear, a group of Pacific islanders will set sail on an exploratory voyage, traveling east in search of new islands to settle. They have no maps, and use their knowledge of the sea, stars, and other elements of nature to find their way. Preparations for the trip take place alongside busy island life. There are boats to build, fish to catch, and centuries of knowledge to pass on from parents to children.

The voyagers have built a large canoe with two hulls, strong enough to travel for many weeks across the ocean.

Pacific Ocean

Double-hulled canoe

Bioluminescence

Fishers

At night, tiny sea organisms emit flashes of light, which can help direct sailors toward land.

Dugout canoe

Adze

Turtle

Shellfish gatherers

 A woman adds bananas to the pile of taro, breadfruit, dried fish, and coconuts she is preparing for the voyagers to take with them.

 These shellfish gatherers wear dresses made of bark cloth. Unlike woven cloth, it is made by pounding the soft inner bark of paper mulberry trees.

Two monumental bulls, symbolizing the power of the Persian king, look down upon those entering the Gate of All Nations.

The Elamite delegation, from the ancient land of Elam on the Persian Gulf, brings a lioness and two cubs, archers' bows, and daggers as gifts.

NEW YEAR FESTIVAL
Persepolis, Persian Empire, c. 480 BCE

It is the New Year festival of Nowruz, and the wealth and power of the Persian king is on dazzling display. People from every corner of the empire have traveled to the Persian ceremonial capital, Persepolis, where the royal family is in residence for the occasion. At the heart of the festivities is a spectacular procession, when thousands of delegates from every subject nation climb the great stairs and enter the Apadana Palace, bringing with them precious gifts as tribute to the king.

Gate of All Nations

Throne Hall

Royal bodyguards

Bull sculpture

Double staircase

Ethiopian delegation

Persian dignitaries

Elamite delegation

Water channel

Persian noble

Royal gardens

A royal bodyguard stands at attention. Today, his weapons are for show, signifying strength and power.

A Persian noble hurries to join the dignitaries at the foot of the staircase. His fine chariot shows his status.

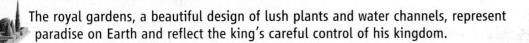
The royal gardens, a beautiful design of lush plants and water channels, represent paradise on Earth and reflect the king's careful control of his kingdom.

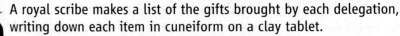
A royal scribe makes a list of the gifts brought by each delegation, writing down each item in cuneiform on a clay tablet.

 At the king's request, Babylonian artisans created friezes of green and yellow glazed tiles to decorate the tops of the ceremonial buildings.

Each column in the west portico stands 82 ft (25 m) high and is topped by a carved stone capital in the shape of two lion heads.

Fortification walls

Apadana Palace

Decorative frieze

Royal women

Subject nation delegations

Seasonal camp

Scribe

Indian delegation

The Ethiopian delegation brings okapis, an elephant tusk, and bowls to showcase their metalworking skills.

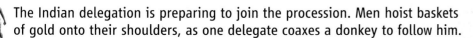 The Indian delegation is preparing to join the procession. Men hoist baskets of gold onto their shoulders, as one delegate coaxes a donkey to follow him.

 When visiting Persepolis, both the king's attendants and delegates from subject nations stay in an enormous tented camp below the palace complex.

Market stalls selling similar goods cluster together. Among the perfume stalls, a merchant helps an enslaved woman choose a scent for her mistress.

Enslaved men begin to rope off an area for an ostracism vote, at which citizens will decide whether to send an unpopular fellow citizen into exile.

A DAY IN THE AGORA
Athens, Ancient Greece, c. 420 BCE

In recent decades, Athens has become the dominant Greek city-state, known for its powerful military, skillful artists, and great thinkers. This is a democracy, so Athenian citizens—and therefore not women, enslaved people, or foreign-born men—decide how Athens should be run. At the heart of city life is the *agora*, a vast space surrounded by fine sanctuaries, shops, law courts, and government buildings. Here, citizens gather daily to buy goods; worship; tackle political, legal, and philosophical questions; or simply to chat.

A commander of the Athenian cavalry inspects some horses to decide whether they are fit to go to war.

Following his trial at the nearby law courts, a man celebrates with his friends, delighted he has been found innocent.

Plane trees planted for shade

Fountain House

Horse inspection

Perfume stall

Ostracism pen

Enslaved men

Marketplace

Jurors

Athenian citizens

Enslaved woman shopping for her mistress

Marketplace official

Members of Athenian Council

 A merchant uses a standard Athenian measuring cup to pour out nuts for a customer, watched closely by a marketplace official.

 These councillors are among 500—50 from each tribe—chosen by lot to govern Athens. They decide which matters Athenian citizens should vote on.

The Fountain House is busiest before sunrise, when Athenian women come to fetch water for their household, taking care not to be seen by men.

Two friends step into the *Aiakeion*, an open-air sanctuary dedicated to King Aiakos of Aegina, to worship this hero of fairness and justice.

Parthenon

Acropolis

Temple of Athena Nike

South Stoa (colonnade)

Aiakeion (open-air sanctuary)

ocrates

Scythian soldier

Line of citizens

Statue of Eponymous Heroes

Each statue represents one of the 10 tribes of Athens. Every Athenian citizen is a member of one of these tribes.

Citizens line up to read public notices posted for their tribe. Will they be called up to the army today?

 The philosopher Socrates challenges a fellow citizen to question his own opinions, drawing a small crowd curious to listen to their discussion.

 Scythian soldiers captured while at war with Athens now serve the city as enslaved people. They work as police officers, easily recognized by their distinctive clothing.

Leading the charge are the awe-inspiring war elephants, powerful enough to cross rivers, trample opponents, and cause panic among enemy lines.

A horseman sounds a long note using a conch shell, signaling to the ranks of the cavalry that it is time to advance.

A CLASH OF MIGHTY ARMIES
Indus River Valley, Mauryan Empire, c. 305 BCE

It is nearly 20 years since Chandragupta Maurya unified hundreds of separate kingdoms in ancient India under the Mauryan Empire with the support of his mentor, Chanakya. In that time, they have built up a huge, highly organized army made up of infantry, cavalry, chariots, and war elephants. When a powerful Greek commander, Seleucus I Nicator, gathers his army in the Indus River Valley, planning to seize Mauryan territory, Chandragupta meets the Seleucid army with the full force of Mauryan military might.

A Greek horse rears up and unseats his rider, startled by the terrifying wall of elephants bearing down on them.

A Mauryan spy among Greek ranks races to pass on enemy battle secrets to his own side, hoping he will not be discovered.

Indus River

Greek cavalry

Seleucus I Nicator

Macedonian phalanx

A soldier proudly carries the imperial banner bearing a peacock feather emblem—peacocks were associated both with warfare and with the Maurya.

One of the emperor's team of female bodyguards shoots a poison-tipped arrow at a Greek soldier. She is committed to protecting Chandragupta's life.

A foot soldier charges forward, mace in hand, knowing there is strength in numbers—the Mauryan infantry is 600,000 strong.

The Mauryan encampment has been designed to provide well-organized support, with thousands of attendants to cater to the soldiers' and animals' needs.

A chariot struggles to advance as its wheels sink into the mud, making it harder for the riders to attack or defend themselves.

Chanakya watches the battle unfold from his chariot, advising Chandragupta on how to defeat the enemy.

Mauryan encampment

Mauryan cavalry

Mauryan infantry

Chanakya

Chandragupta Maurya

Female bodyguard

Mauryan chariots

Archers

Elephant driver

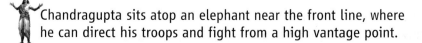

Chandragupta sits atop an elephant near the front line, where he can direct his troops and fight from a high vantage point.

This soldier is among thousands of horsemen who make up the Mauryan cavalry, armed with lances to thrust and throw at the enemy.

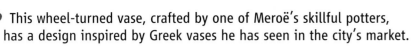

This wheel-turned vase, crafted by one of Meroë's skillful potters, has a design inspired by Greek vases he has seen in the city's market.

Until her son comes of age, the kandake (queen) will rule Kush in his place. She will also complete her husband's pyramid and offering chapel.

Rows of mourners carry palm fronds, which they believe will bring long life to the king in the afterlife.

Among the gifts are statues of Egyptian and Kushite gods, reflecting centuries of close ties between the kingdoms.

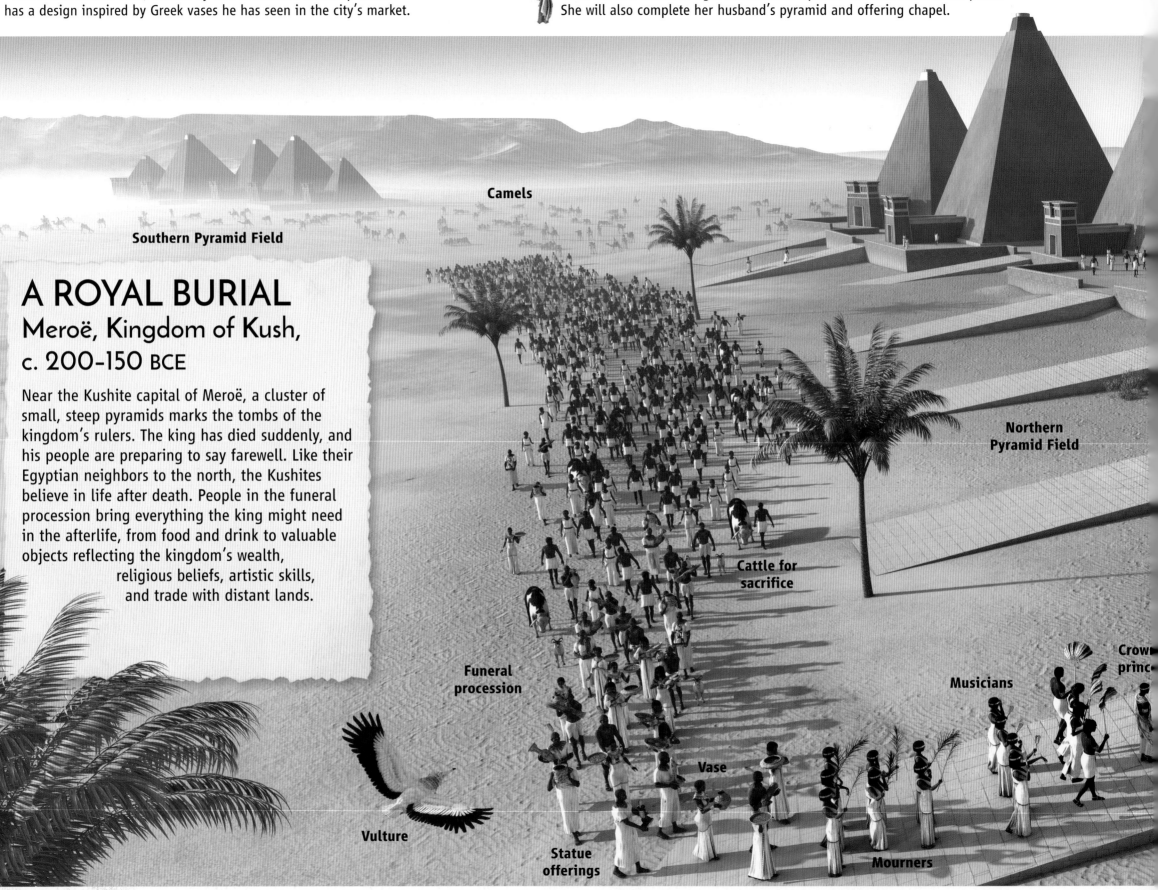

Southern Pyramid Field

Camels

A ROYAL BURIAL
Meroë, Kingdom of Kush, c. 200–150 BCE

Near the Kushite capital of Meroë, a cluster of small, steep pyramids marks the tombs of the kingdom's rulers. The king has died suddenly, and his people are preparing to say farewell. Like their Egyptian neighbors to the north, the Kushites believe in life after death. People in the funeral procession bring everything the king might need in the afterlife, from food and drink to valuable objects reflecting the kingdom's wealth, religious beliefs, artistic skills, and trade with distant lands.

Northern Pyramid Field

Cattle for sacrifice

Funeral procession

Musicians

Crown prince

Vase

Vulture

Statue offerings

Mourners

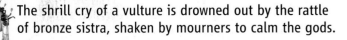 The shrill cry of a vulture is drowned out by the rattle of bronze sistra, shaken by mourners to calm the gods.

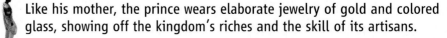 Like his mother, the prince wears elaborate jewelry of gold and colored glass, showing off the kingdom's riches and the skill of its artisans.

Artisans are carving the reliefs decorating the previous queen's chapel—they show her receiving offerings, protected by the winged goddess Isis.

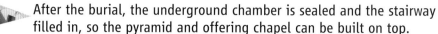
After the burial, the underground chamber is sealed and the stairway filled in, so the pyramid and offering chapel can be built on top.

Using a shaduf, workers haul stone to the top of the pyramid. A bronze capstone will be placed on top.

Scribes record the burial offerings using a new Kushite alphabet inspired by Egyptian hieroglyphs.

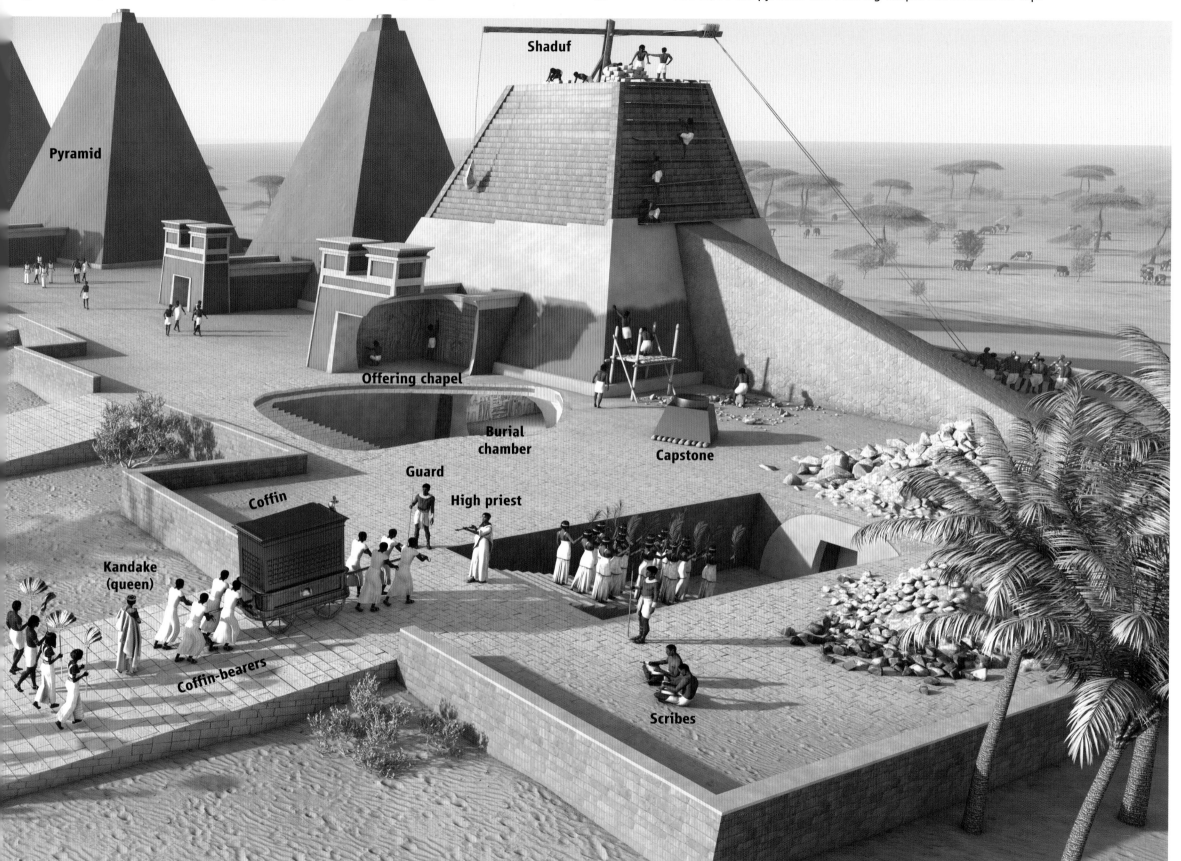

Pyramid

Shaduf

Offering chapel

Burial chamber

Capstone

Guard

Coffin

High priest

Kandake (queen)

Coffin-bearers

Scribes

This guard's spearhead was made in Meroë's metalworks. Making and selling iron weapons and gold jewelry has helped make the kingdom rich.

Perfume scents the air as the high priest pauses to make an offering of incense before entering the underground burial chamber.

A brand new warship sets off, fitted with a bronze battering ram to attack Roman ships, and brightly painted eyes to ward off evil.

The goddess Tanit is Carthage's chief protector, and her symbol appears on buildings and stelae across the city.

Carthage's greatest weapons are its speedy warships with three rows of oars powered by up to 300 oarsmen.

With wide decks and deep hulls, these merchant ships are perfect for stowing away large amounts of cargo.

Temple of Tanit

Warship

Rectangular harbor

Merchant ship

Glassmaker

Amphorae

 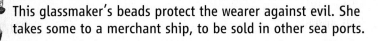

This glassmaker's beads protect the wearer against evil. She takes some to a merchant ship, to be sold in other sea ports.

Sailors begin loading popular Carthaginian exports—barley, fruit, and expensive purple dye and cloth—onto a waiting merchant ship.

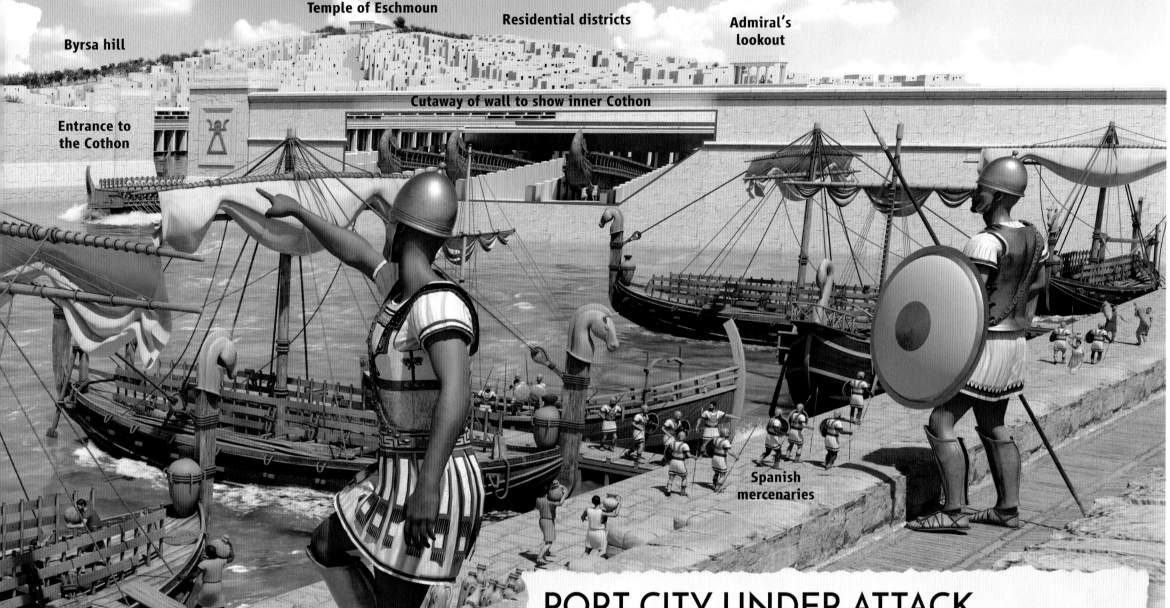

Ship-workers scrape a ship clear of barnacles, knowing they will slow it down and make it harder to escape from the enemy.

The Cothon is a circular harbor for 200 ships, with a round island in the middle. Its high walls help Carthage hide its fleet of warships.

Byrsa hill

Temple of Eschmoun

Residential districts

Admiral's lookout

Entrance to the Cothon

Cutaway of wall to show inner Cothon

Spanish mercenaries

City wall

From his island lookout, the admiral can see any approaching ships beyond the city walls, and sound an alarm if needed.

A city guard alerts his companion to smoke beyond the hill. It is a sign the fighting is getting closer.

PORT CITY UNDER ATTACK
Carthage, Carthaginian Civilization, c. 149–148 BCE

The city-state of Carthage, in North Africa, is under attack from the Romans in the third of the Punic Wars between them. Carthage is fighting to save what is left of its wealthy sea empire. Its twin harbors, hidden from the enemy behind the city walls, keep its hopes alive. While shipbuilders race to build more warships, dozens of merchant ships continue to trade with the city's allies, selling Carthaginian crops and luxuries in return for gold, silver, and foreign soldiers.

These men carry pots of gold from West Africa and silver from Spain—valuable metals Carthage can use to buy help from foreign soldiers.

These soldiers have just arrived from Spain. They bring their own weapons, and are being paid good money to help Carthage fight the Romans.

24

Gates like this control who enters and leaves the Han Empire. Massive walls, made of earth and reeds, defend the northern frontier.

An official makes notes on bamboo slips, calculating how much the travelers need to pay to bring their goods into the empire.

Merchants bring jade found in Central Asia, knowing that for the Han, it is more valuable than gold.

This Han merchant is selling Chinese silk. No one outside China knows how to make silk, so he will be paid well.

Gate

Marketplace

Jade

Silk

Merchant

Imperial representative

Han soldiers

 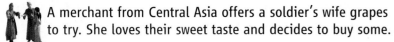
A merchant from Central Asia offers a soldier's wife grapes to try. She loves their sweet taste and decides to buy some.

This imperial representative must take a gift from the emperor to a distant tribe. He stops to swap horses while his attendants wait outside the gate.

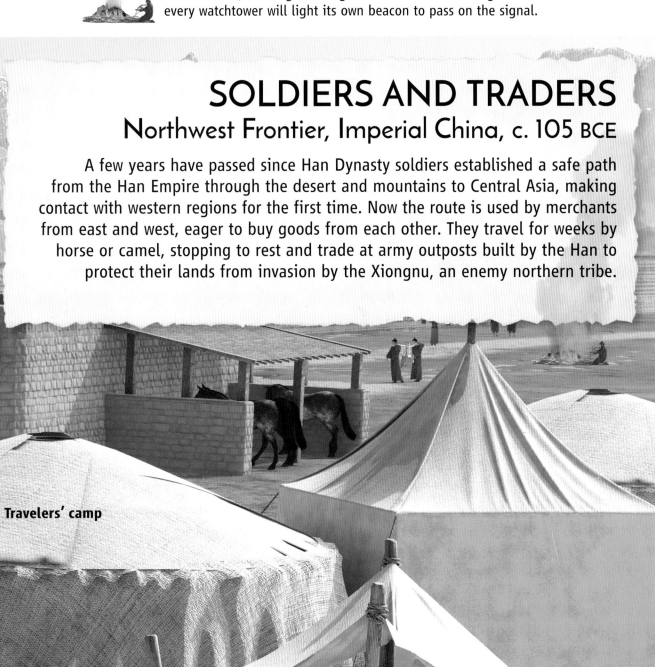

Han soldiers patrolling the desert have captured two Xiongnu raiders, arch enemies of the Han. They worry there may be more nearby.

A beacon is lit, warning of Xiongnu in the area. On seeing the smoke, every watchtower will light its own beacon to pass on the signal.

SOLDIERS AND TRADERS
Northwest Frontier, Imperial China, c. 105 BCE

A few years have passed since Han Dynasty soldiers established a safe path from the Han Empire through the desert and mountains to Central Asia, making contact with western regions for the first time. Now the route is used by merchants from east and west, eager to buy goods from each other. They travel for weeks by horse or camel, stopping to rest and trade at army outposts built by the Han to protect their lands from invasion by the Xiongnu, an enemy northern tribe.

Soldiers may work at outposts for years, so their wives live alongside them. This woman has fetched water from a well.

Two merchants are relaxing. One teaches the other how to play a board game from his homeland.

Watchtower

Defensive wall

Xiongnu raiders

Travelers' camp

Camel

A Han guard questions the leader of the arriving travelers, checking where they are going and what goods they are carrying.

Even in the desert, wild animals roam. These soldiers have trapped a gazelle, and are bringing it back to cook and eat.

The president of the day's races holds a piece of white cloth, which he will use to signal the start of each race.

This Egyptian obelisk dates to the 13th century BCE but was brought to the Circus Maximus in 10 BCE as a trophy of Rome's conquest of Egypt.

Twelve more chariots are already lining up in the starting boxes eager for the next event.

An official waits by the finish line, ready to give a palm frond to the lucky winner of the contest.

A DAY AT THE RACES
Rome, Ancient Rome, c. 100–150 CE

Excitement is building in the Circus Maximus, the largest and most famous stadium in the Roman Empire. A thrilling chariot race is under way, and it feels as if all of Rome has come to watch—from the noblest citizen to the poorest enslaved person. Wearing red, white, green, or blue to show support for their favorite team, the spectators roar as a chariot overturns. The charioteers drive on. They are brave men, ready to risk their lives for prize money.

Obelisk of Augustus

Starting gates

Central barrier

Lap counters

Attendant

Support rider

A boy studying with his tutor looks up from his wax tablet, distracted by the crowd—if only he could watch the race!

A fierce argument breaks out between two men supporting rival teams. One has accused the other's favorite charioteer of cheating.

An official pushes up an egg on a pole to keep track of the number of laps completed. Each race is seven laps—two down, five more to go!

The Roman emperor watches the race from the imperial box, standing up to get a good view of the action.

Imperial palace

Imperial box

Turning posts

Chariot

Four-horse chariot races are the most popular. The chariots are light and fast, but are easily overturned.

The charioteer wears leather strapping to protect his body, and keeps a knife to cut himself free if he gets tangled in the reins.

An attendant turns his head to avoid the flying sand. His job is to rake the track smooth between races.

Each team has a support rider to encourage their contestants. The blue rider urges his teammates to block the green chariot trying to get past.

Sun and rain have caused the temple decoration to flake and fade. An artisan repaints a mask, bringing its bold colors back to life.

 Now that he is 20, the prince is allowed to wear a special headdress. The king, in ceremonial costume, presents the headdress to his son with pride.

A PRINCE COMES OF AGE
Tikal, Maya Civilization, c. 740 CE

Festivities are under way in Tikal, a large city in a powerful Maya city-state, deep in the Central American forest. Today, the ruler's son celebrates his *k'atun*—reaching 20 years old by the Maya calendar. The king is leading a ceremony amid the temples of the city's Great Plaza, where a stela has been carved with a picture of the prince. A ball game tournament has begun, and everyone is looking forward to a day of music, dancing, and feasting.

Farmers bring baskets of maize from fields around the city, using tumpline straps to carry the heaviest loads.

These women are laden with baskets brimming with fruit and vegetables for the feast following the ceremony.

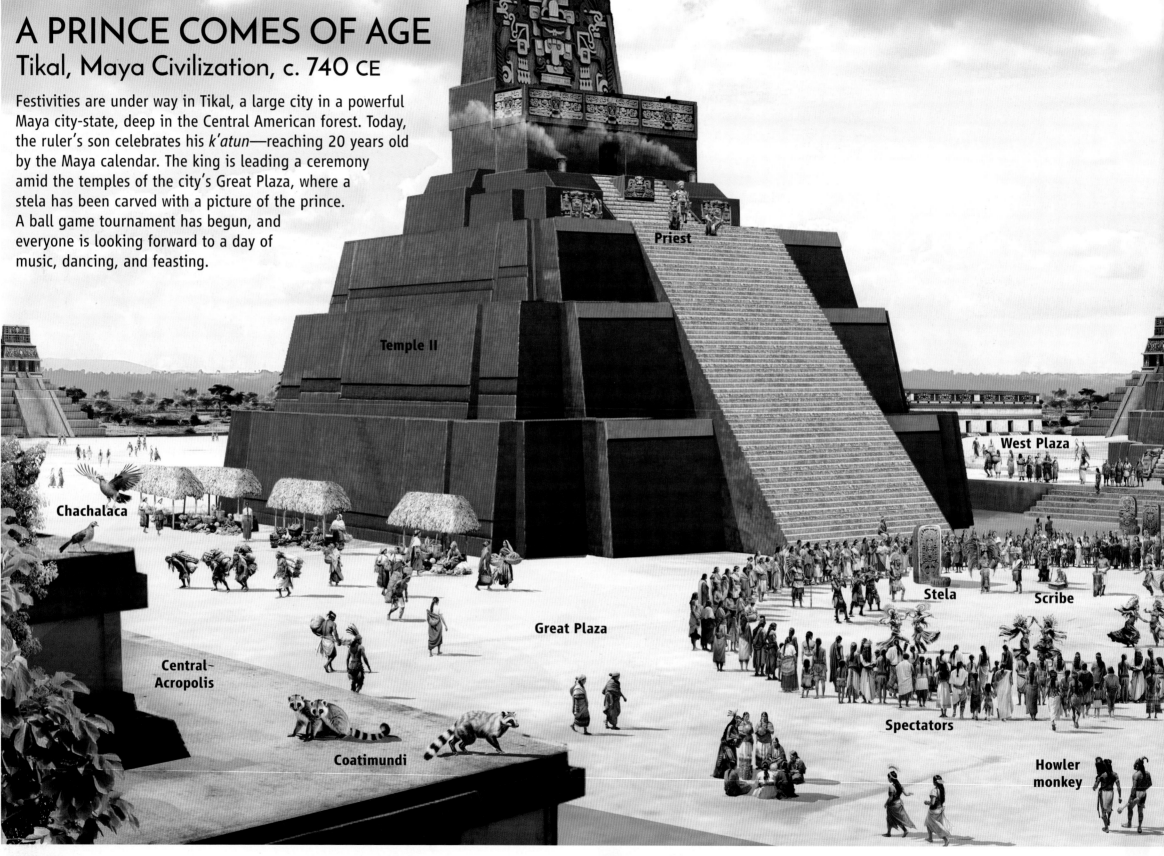

Priest

Temple II

West Plaza

Chachalaca

Stela

Scribe

Great Plaza

Central-Acropolis

Spectators

Coatimundi

Howler monkey

 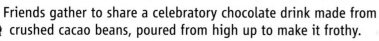 Friends gather to share a celebratory chocolate drink made from crushed cacao beans, poured from high up to make it frothy.

 As the prince accepts his headdress, musicians sound their horns, while dancers stamp their ankle rattles to the rhythm of drums.

A man pauses to lay an offering at an altar before one of the North Acropolis temples, where many earlier rulers are buried.

Like many Maya, this noblewoman loves jewelry. She likes the rich colors of quetzal feathers, pink spondylus shell, and green jadeite best of all.

North Acropolis

Temple I

Scarlet macaw

 This proud warrior has brought his fierce animal headdress and spear to show his high status.

 A ball player knocks the ball over the line with his hips—using his hands or feet is against the rules.

Ball court

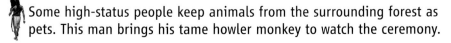 Some high-status people keep animals from the surrounding forest as pets. This man brings his tame howler monkey to watch the ceremony.

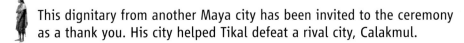 This dignitary from another Maya city has been invited to the ceremony as a thank you. His city helped Tikal defeat a rival city, Calakmul.

PIECING TOGETHER THE PAST

Archaeology is about finding out how people in the past lived by studying what they left behind, from the tools they used to the art they created. Here are some of the objects that have helped archaeologists piece together a picture of what life was like for the peoples in this book.

see page 6

Ka-aper is depicted as well-fed, suggesting he was also well paid.

Statue of Ka-aper

The Pyramid Builders' Town: Ancient Egypt

This wooden statue was carved around 4,500 years ago, when the pyramids of Giza were built. It shows Ka-aper, an Egyptian priest and scribe. He carries a staff as a symbol of his official role.

A Thriving Community: Caral Civilization

Caral people did not bake clay to make pottery, but they did mold clay figures to use in rituals. When constructing buildings, they often buried figurines like this one in the walls as offerings.

Caral men may have worn their hair in this style.

Clay figurine

see page 8

The blue lapis lazuli was brought from Afghanistan, while the red carnelian came from western India.

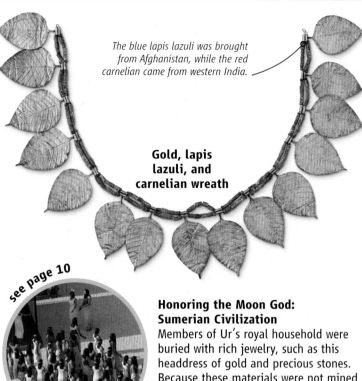

Gold, lapis lazuli, and carnelian wreath

see page 10

Honoring the Moon God: Sumerian Civilization

Members of Ur's royal household were buried with rich jewelry, such as this headdress of gold and precious stones. Because these materials were not mined near Ur, the Sumerians brought them in from Asia by boat.

Digital reconstruction of a Lapita bowl

The patterns are similar to modern Polynesian tattoo designs.

see page 12

Ocean Explorers: Lapita Culture

This bowl, with its geometric pattern, is typical of the decorative pottery made by the Lapita. Patterns were pressed into the wet clay using a variety of tools with toothlike edges, called dentate stamps.

see page 14

The golden jewelry is a sign of the Persian Empire's wealth.

New Year Festival: Persian Empire

These colorful glazed tiles decorated the Persian kings' seasonal palace at Susa (in modern-day Iran). They show the clothing royal guards wore and the weapons they carried, while suggesting the strength of the Persian army.

Glazed tiles from Susa Palace

see page 16

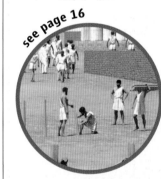

A Day in the Agora: Ancient Greece

These broken pottery pieces are ostracism votes. Athenian citizens used them like modern paper, scratching down the name of a citizen they wanted to banish. Whoever had the most votes was banned from Athens for 10 years.

Ostracism votes

The name on these votes is Themistocles, an Athenian general.

Relief from Sanchi showing the Siege of Kushinagar

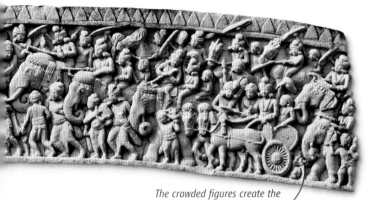

The crowded figures create the impression of a large army.

see page 18

A Clash of Mighty Armies: Mauryan Empire

Few items have survived from Mauryan times, but this panel from a Buddhist monument built by the Mauryan emperor Ashoka (Chandragupta Maurya's grandson), shows the ancient army made up of elephants, chariots, cavalry, and infantry.

A winged goddess decorates the hinge of the bracelet.

Royal bracelet

see page 20

A Royal Burial: Kingdom of Kush

The Kingdom of Kush had rich gold mines and its goldsmiths became experts at creating wonderful jewelry. This gold and enamel bracelet belonged to Queen Amanishakheto, and was found hidden inside her pyramid at Meroë.

---

see page 22

Port City Under Attack: Carthaginian Civilization

Carthage was famous for making and trading luxury goods, including glass charms such as these head-shaped pendants. People believed that beads with blue eyes would protect them by reflecting evil back onto any evil-doer.

Head-shaped beads usually had curly hair and beards.

Glass head pendants

Soldiers and Traders: Imperial China

These clay figures are replica Han Dynasty soldiers in uniform. They were among 2,500 figurines discovered in the tomb of a Western Han general near the ancient Han capital of Chang'an (Xian in modern-day China).

Clay soldiers

see page 24

Traces of paint show the soldiers' uniforms and shields were brown and red.

Mosaic of the Circus Maximus

The picture is made of thousands of tiny, colored stone squares.

see page 26

A Day at the Races: Ancient Rome

The races at the Circus Maximus in Rome were so popular that they appear in several Roman artworks. This mosaic from a villa in Sicily shows a four-horse chariot racing toward an official with a palm frond.

The dancers wear fantastic costumes, including giant, crablike claws.

Painting of musicians and dancers

A Prince Comes of Age: Maya Civilization

This wall painting from the Maya city of Bonampak (in modern-day Mexico) gives a good idea of what Maya celebrations were like during the Classic Period: full of music; dancing; and bold, colorful costumes.

see page 28

GLOSSARY

Achaemenid
The name of the family who ruled ancient Persia between c. 550 and c. 334 BCE.

Agora
The ancient Greek word for a public space used for gatherings and market activity.

Ancestor
A person who lived in the past, and who is a distant relative of people who are alive today.

Archaeology
The study of objects and remains left behind by peoples of the past, in order to reveal their history.

Artisan
A skilled craftsperson producing things by hand.

Athenian citizen
A free, adult man born in Athens, with Athenian parents, in ancient Greece.

BCE
A term meaning "Before the Common Era," placed after a date to show it happened before year 0, which is the start of the "Common Era" (CE).

Bitumen
An oily, sticky substance used as cement in ancient times but now used to make roads.

Buddhist
A believer in, or something related to, Buddhism, a religion that began in ancient India.

Capital
In a building, the part at the top of a column that supports the structure resting on it.

CE
Abbreviation for "Common Era," used in dates (see BCE).

Ceremonial
Something used for official, religious, or social events.

Citizen
A person who belongs to a city or a bigger community, such as a country, and has certain rights.

City-state
A city, and its surrounding territory, that has its own independent government.

Civilization
The culture and way of life of people living together in a complex society.

Culture
The customs, beliefs, and behavior shared by a society.

Cuneiform
A system of writing using wedge-shaped marks, first used in Sumer then adopted by other civilizations.

Deity
A god or goddess.

Delegate
A person chosen to represent a country or other group. Several delegates can form a delegation.

Democracy
A system of government where decisions are made by the people being governed, or by people representing them.

Dignitary
A person of high rank.

Dynasty
A family ruling a country for successive generations.

Empire
A group of lands or peoples under the rule of a single government or person (an emperor).

Enslaved people
A person who is owned by another person as their property. Enslaved people have no rights and work with no pay.

Exile
To send someone into exile is to banish a citizen from their own city or country as punishment.

Export
The sale of goods and services to another country. The opposite of imports.

Gourd
A round fruit with a hard shell that can be used as a container.

Government
A group of people governing a country, often (but not always) elected to do so.

Hieroglyphics
An ancient Egyptian system of writing in which pictures represented sounds, objects, and ideas.

Imperial
Of or relating to an empire.

Indigenous peoples
The first people to live in a particular place.

K'atun
20 Maya years, where one year is 360 days.

Khipu
A counting tool used by Caral and later Andean civilizations. It was made of colored cords that could be knotted to record information.

Loom
A frame used to weave thread into cloth.

Lot
To choose by lot is to choose someone or something from a group at random.

Mace
A blunt, club-like weapon used to hit an enemy.

Macedonian phalanx
A battle formation made up of closely packed rows of foot soldiers armed with long pikes.

Mentor
Someone who provides a less experienced person with advice and support.

Merchant
A person who buys or sells goods.

Mesopotamia
The region of modern-day Iraq lying between the Tigris and Euphrates rivers, where the earliest civilizations began.

Mourner
A person attending the funeral of a friend or relative.

Noble
A member of the nobility or aristocracy, with more rights and privileges than people who were peasants or merchants.

Offering
Something given to a god or gods as an act of worship.

Ostracism
In ancient Greece, the act of banishing someone from their community.

Pharaoh
A title given to a king in ancient Egypt.

Philosopher
A person who thinks and writes seriously about the meaning of life.

Quarry
A place where rocks are dug or hacked out from the ground.

Relief
A style of stone carving in which the shapes appear to stand out from the flat surface.

Ritual
A set of words and/or actions that are always performed the same way, for example in a religious ceremony.

Sacred
Considered holy, and with religious significance, possibly related to a god or goddess.

Sanctuary
A place for worship or that offers protection.

Scribe
Before printing was invented, a person whose job was to write and make copies of official documents.

Scythian
A person from Scythia, a historic region north of ancient Persia.

Shaduf
A wooden, seesaw-like device with a weight at one end, used to help lift heavy items such as water or stone.

Shicra bag
A strong net bag made of woven reeds, filled with stones, and used to fill walls during construction.

Sistrum (plural sistra)
A handheld, metal rattle-like instrument used in ancient Egypt and ancient Rome.

Stela (plural stelae)
An upright stone monument, often carved with an inscription. Stelae were often set up by rulers to honor people or gods, or mark a tomb.

Subject nation
A country that is controlled by the ruler of another country, for example as part of an empire.

Temple
A building for religious worship or ceremonies.

Territory
A geographic area that has come under the control of a government.

Trade
The buying, selling, or exchanging of goods or services between people.

Tribute
A valuable gift given by one ruler to another to show that they recognize the ruler receiving the tribute as the greater power.

Tumpline
A strap worn around the forehead to support the carrying of heavy loads on the back.

Wheel-turned
Refers to pottery that has been made by shaping the clay on a spinning disk, called a potter's wheel.

Ziggurat
A type of stepped, brick temple building found in the main cities of the Sumerian, Assyrian, and Babylonian civilizations.

ACKNOWLEDGMENTS

For Smithsonian Enterprises:
Avery Naughton, Licensing Coordinator, Paige Towler, Editorial Lead, Jill Corcoran, Senior Director, Licensed Publishing, Brigid Corcoran, Vice President of New Business and Licensing, Carol LeBlanc, President

Smithsonian reviewer:
J. Keith Wilson, Curator of Ancient Chinese Art, Freer Gallery of Art and Arthur M. Sackler Gallery

The Smithsonian name and logo are registered trademarks of the Smithsonian.

Dorling Kindersley would like to thank:
Binta Jallow for additional editing; Simon Mumford for additional design; Carron Brown for proofreading; Sumedha Chopra for picture research; Steve Crozier for creative retouching; SJC Illustrations for additional illustrations; Elizabeth Wise for the index; Mik Gates and Rob Perry for visualization; Harri Kettunen for additional advice on the Maya civilization

The publisher would like to thank the following for their kind permission to reproduce their photographs:

(Key: a-above; b-below/bottom; c-center; f-far; l-left; r-right; t-top)

2 Alamy Stock Photo: Archive PL (br); Giuseppe Cipriani (tc). **Dreamstime.com:** Wirestock (cr). **3 Alamy Stock Photo:** Mike P Shepherd (clb). **Dreamstime.com:** Imtmphoto (cra); Alvar German Vilela (tl); Sergey Mayorov (tr); Radiokafka (bc); Kelpfish (crb). **Getty Images / iStock:** Fabianodp (tc); Kum Seong Wan (cr). **Getty Images:** Christian SAPPA Gamma-Rapho (cb). **8 Dorling Kindersley:** Tatton Park (clb). **12 Dreamstime.com:** Guido Amrein (crb); Susan Peterson (cb). **18–19 123RF.com:** fedbul. **Dreamstime.com:** Okea (water, splash); Konstantin Sutyagin (smoke). Fotolia: Okea (water splash, blue water). **22–23 Dreamstime.com:** Wessel Cirkel (ocean); Michalakis Ppalis; Werte (ripples); Kmiragaya (water). **26–27 123RF.com:** Maria Itina (b). **28 Getty Images / iStock:** PDerrett / E+ (bc, c). **30 Alamy Stock Photo:** funkyfood London Paul Williams (tr); Vita exclusive (br). **Bridgeman Images:** Sandro Vannini (c). **Dorling Kindersley:** University of Pennsylvania Museum of Archaeology and Anthropology (cr). **Science Photo Library:** Pasquale Sorrentino (bc). **31 Alamy Stock Photo:** ART Collection (crb); Peter Horree (clb); The Print Collector (ca); YongXin Zhang (bc). **Dreamstime.com:** EPhotocorp (tl). **Getty Images:** DEA / Archivio J. Lange (tr)

All other images © Dorling Kindersley